this feels like a suicide mission

Jordan Denae Snider

this feels like a suicide mission

yesterdaysmile press

Copyright © 2014 Jordan Denae Snider. All rights reserved.

All rights reserved. This book or any portion thereof may not be reproduced or used in any manner whatsoever without the express written permission of the publisher except for the use of brief quotations in a book review or scholarly journal.

First Printing: 2014

yesterdaysmile press LLC 2014 ISBN 978-0-692-25843-9

Cover Design: Betty Schulte
Cover Photo: Drew Snider
Edited: Amanda Rumble, Betty Schulte
Type is Times New Roman
Printed in the United States of America

Portions of this book will be donated to National Alliance on Mental Health (NAMI). nami.org

in memoriam
Jordan Denae Snider
1992 - 2011

Contents

11.	yesteryear bleeds
13.	empty eternities
15.	lucid obscurities
17.	consumption, lengthy in decision
21.	the up rise in the night, I can still see the sunrise
23.	at the desk of yesterday inscriptions
25.	sick and tired of silence
28.	future awake, past dreaming, present awake
30.	breakingout
33.	undead last
34.	winged undertakers
35.	head against the wall
36.	make it so
38.	speakers and scotch tape
39.	manic-depression
41.	a sitcom called CRASHE
43.	complications
46.	likely a little looming leverage
47.	breaking the pattern
49.	last stake
51.	speaking to nature
54.	switch course
58.	from the other side
60.	hopeless
61.	one present
62.	under upheaval / black morning risen
64.	empyrean demons
67.	liars
68.	harbored harmony
70.	green sweatshirt walking
71.	this feels like a suicide mission
72.	borderline star
74.	number three
76.	No Title Necessary, But It's Still a Good Accessory
77.	stages of sight
78.	bachelors bewitched
80.	gypsy
81.	so funny, closed but no closure
83.	i thought i knew, but mood rings never lie
85.	covered
87.	view 6
89.	this is an outstanding POS
91.	sea legs on a plane

Contents continued

93.	Prozac attack
95.	awake and sleeping
97.	dirty pop and TNT [timeBOMB]
99.	dear Lightning
101.	without
103.	sunken treasure
105.	i want to be hidden in the stars
108.	racing
110.	break/through, a symphony in two parts
112.	there's a time and a place for everything
114.	un-adapted
115.	a foundation for failure
117.	mistrust, misthought
119.	arsenal assets
121.	courage in tour [escaping entourage]
123.	tic tac toe
124.	the alchemist
126.	close to THE END

this feels like a suicide mission

"I was stuck once.
But after a long time I was able to move forward,
first feebly, then confidently.
I am now motivated by the desire to never become
trapped again."

Jordan D. Snider

yesteryear bleeds

but my skin isn't vintage
and it doesn't rust
my skin isn't floral based
wallpaper or heaven laced
dust

but it still remembers the rip's crusade
down that purple lamp shade
but it still remembers the coke stain on the couch
the green carpet, the black and white tv
it still remembers who i used to be

back when the days were stringing along
a bracelet of suns and moons lifelong
where the trees lined up, chopped down
dreams started walking by
eyes closed satisfaction
all just a misconception's night

but my skin isn't vintage
and it doesn't rust
but the wrinkles are starting
and i'm starting to bust

out again into the crowds
finally leaving that old couch
walking amidst strangers
though still paranoid of the dangers
hearing the sounds of terror
in silence and dogs barking

but my skin isn't vintage
and it doesn't rust

my skin isn't floral based
wallpaper or heaven laced
dust

but it still remembers the first kiss upon his lips
the break -- the break something i'd just take
but it still remembers holding out for something more
but giving, giving in begging for open doors

but my skin isn't vintage
and it doesn't rust
but it takes all the cuts
and the burns appear, there are scars here

so no, there aren't any polaroid's
of the car i crash and drove
the explosion on the stove
on the table, sitting pretty

but my skin recalls the ugly
way he disappeared
the way he almost-loved me,
the way he never made it clear

but my skin isn't vintage
even after all these years
and it doesn't rust
my skin isn't floral based
wallpaper or heaven laced
manic lust but i'm going on
and going off
collecting cobwebs and collecting dust

empty eternities

emotion reigns down
like every tear drop falling from
and drowning in red wine
copper blood and salt
burning bipolar breakdowns
lemon juice stings ill-willed
brings the still
clock stops
too tired to waste time with me
let's pretend let's always
let's never end
hollow bones
suck the poison from my bones
inject it straight into my veins
honing zoning
nervous fever sweating heart
its a dynamic duo
wearing tomorrow like a stolen jacket
razors ready to rape
once wasn't enough
make sure it's deep enough to scar
devout to bad choices
law gone forever raw
perception
blind with predator
deaf with prey
only a million shards to steal my heart away
maybe mirror
Misery's escape
years no longer
they're oh so longer
contortionist confidence
decay rot

beautiful but not
given grief
lonely belief
wretched relief
a door
memory
dark with graffiti
positivity swirling down the toilet
like a dead goldfish
what an ugly goldfish
rubber banded heart barely mended
quick turns dead ends decorated
with ivy and barbed wire
astute liar
eternity is only for not so pretty endings
i have no fire exit

lucid obscurities

salivating but throat dry, and i realized
i belong to a community that doesn't recognize
me when i walk by,
neighbors that have archives of images
fragmented memories
of a girl, disheveled
that cleaned up but still doesn't comprehend
her own identity

carpeted, occasionally yours
though never comfortable in you:
a home that loves me more
than i ever have, than i ever could
love it back
just let this ordinary day
stop regretting me
;i don't care if it does belong to me..

silence building, coughing up
instilled fragrances
like "welcome home hash",
a time bomb of drugged up mornings
crashing down after too many
hand-washing attempts

the blood never leaves
the memory never recedes
admitting personal disagreements-
underdeveloped majesties
are just statues never finished//
give up again and again,
wasting your time sipping on
dreams

listing serious symptoms off a mental health pamphlet
cat and girl sit together calmly, searching for nothing more
than what they have,
but the cat is dead and the girl is just
a second away from
taking a long drive off a short pier

no more no more, every direction from you
warped skin, burns from a friendly fascist freer fire
face down-face down--face Down.
possible errors admitting once again
into a cold dark sea
withered rising, syringes casting heavy glances into
a girl in a hole called home residency

heartbeat, a rhythm she once heard in
a song she once loved
causes without the drive
never come true, back to being you
no longer valid yesterday
me/enemies
same girl who walked out that door

and my neighbor asked
"what did they do to you"
pleas, begging on my knees
"sir, i've never met you"
crawling back to
archives never seen through
another underdeveloped majesty's eyes

...and after everything,
i still love you...

consumption, lengthy in decision

maybe if i forgot what matters
those words that go pitter patter
and play at my heart strings
this would be easier
i would breathe in freer

knowing that everything
my fingers type just makes me angry
jealous of the betters that i could be i
should by now, know it's time to
let go, and forget

it's time to forget that
writing is what's the matter
when i begin to sink
and pretend that i don't think
about the things that hover
in and out of average existence

i remember a friend that would share dark
and beautiful conversations, with me but
now I'm just useless
smothered by the idea that
i could be something, but i am
i am not

and the days continue on
and my world becomes more
and more average
more and more unremarkable

there were others around
and once i can remember being told

i love, and sometimes even you
but now they've all left
because there's nothing special left in me
nothing special left

and all i can stutter
is and and and
but but but
why why why

in my mind, questions get the best of me
haven't i gotten good at
speaking in tongues
haven't i gotten great at
leaving the loves
aren't i the best at
leading a lie?
but the questions just lead to the worst of me

/
i think tomorrow is the worst
best thing I've ever been given
i think that it was better
when i could write down
all the twisted stories
that could fix the lows and highs

but now that there's nothing,
it seems the hole is getting bigger
and this is the worst way to describe
all that's happened to me

but this is all i can muster
this is my last, but my better

/
healthy watches over
the razor is still in the shower
but i take it out sometimes
just to remember
all i was
all i could be

all that i never never knew
you look at me
as i ask myself who,
i couldn't answer
and neither could you
so who, i was, who, i am
stays in the darkest blue

they tell me i should be thankful
for all the steps I've taken
for how easily i found the path
after being stuck for so very long
i should be aware
that i am better

and I am aware
that i am better,
the milligrams tell me every day
but somehow i just feel
more and more
out of focus

but somehow i feel
more and more
useless

and it's not getting
any clearer

that I'm not in between
but I'm not on either extreme

I've become lost in the nightmare
i once thought was a dream

so now i wonder why
the reason i used to want to die
it seems to me that
the worst only used to be the best damn reason

because now in today's tepid season
all the bests seem to make
the worst damn reason
to need to cry

the up rise in night; I can still meet the sunrise

seek me when I'm lost
forgive me when I'm found
it is not water in which I drown

searching for relief
asking for directions from strangers:
lovers without hearts
dreamers that can't sleep
blind optimists that can't see the light of day
though none of these can help me on my way
we go together; lost souls scraping our knees on the pavement
seeking our own secular salvations

seek me when I'm lost
forgive me when I'm found
it is not water in which I drown

the moon is my lamp,
helping me to write my story,
I follow it so it's light will protect me
allowing darkness to hold me,
but not consume me

sentenced to numbness or a life of mania and depression
sacrificing happiness for my own sick oppression
does it make you feel better to be my redemption?

seek me when I'm lost
forgive me when I'm found
it is not water in which I drown

creating horrors
enemies and fiends

paranoia stays to accompany me
in the darkness, it's thickness chokes me
with the loudest silence ever heard
still can't forget the sound of a dying bird

seek me when I'm lost
forgive me when I'm found
it is not water in which I drown

I am weak
faithfully returning to dead ends;
blinking headlights/
please catch my attention
before I give in and give up
before I unite with the dead renegades

seek me when I'm lost
forgive me when I'm found
it is not water in which I drown

at the desk of yesterday inscriptions

hide me under memories
and take away inhibitions
super-glued to my soul
rip it into pieces
i'll never be whole
when there's still a vacancy in me

let my heart heal-
inscribed into my skin
written from pens
-all love is strained
and drains thought
until common sense
dreams fitfully

throw me into the lion's cage
rage is only a small fraction of
what keeps me alive
but cowardice is what keeps me here
at the crossroads of sanity
i fear progression i fear regression
so i stay immobile

blanket me with addiction
barbed sheets in a bed of poison
another affliction
all choices i make
fail me considerably
mistakes are great when
you feel nothing is left to win

lose me under pools of blood
let me swim around remembering

everything i want to forget
lose me under pools of lethality
cleaning my insides slow enough
to play one more game
of sorry

sick and tired of silence

shoulders shaking
hallucinations sit in the doorway
cackling at my pathetic attempt
to make them disappear

insides dancing
in fear of mistakenly killing something beautiful
i only rip apart my soul
my skin is red battered and bleeding
my eyeliner is trying to run away
and neither hide the monster living inside me

mind mistaken
another ninety words of misinterpretation
of random cogitation
consideration of the faulty
walking in squares unsuccessfully
they always seem to be circles
perfected in their no corner values

pick a side
the hidden frown found in the corner
of the picture
the attention-whored master of disaster
smiles while taken hostage for an hour
of dismal desire

mind blowing
another whispered goodbye
hello i told you so
don't you ever wonder what i do all day
faking all consciousness
all you have to see is a liability

and you're happy

eyes tearing
tearing out my hair
screeching in exasperation
past tense is all i know
but i'll lie to you so not to let it show

STOP
all the madness inside of me
let it fly away against the wind
in another fitful sleep goes away
everything i meant to say
but never did

i never did say
that it wasn't her but me
i never did say
that i wasn't okay
i never did say
STOP
you'll hurt yourself some day
and i never did say
HELP

i never did say
my prayers
and i won't start today
but believe me it'll all be okay
i don't need a god to make it all go away

in the midst of madness
all the beauty in the world
is multiplied by thirty-seven
divided by seven and then added to eleven
    but always is subtracted from you

i'm broken but buying scotch tape and Band-Aids
i'm small but buying stilts and top hats
i'm me but buying love and masks
i'm dying but buying
one more chance to say..

future awake, past dreaming, present awake

stomach lurching
pumped
pill by pill
swallowed the thrill

smile
all these things I think…
you can't see
because I smile

sadly, it's not the craziest idea
it seems rational to me, at the oddest of times
all these other dreams I keep
all sound ridiculous
impossible to me

the meaning of thirty seven
asking a kitten how to fly a kite
asking a blind man how to turn off light
hoping a window will show me the way
boredom reaching and overdosing
melting melancholy

a widow of past mistakes
taking
talking word for word the last night
spilling

shaking
biting nails
grinding teeth
maybe this will make belief

witnessing
dead bodies that talk
and snakes that scare all happiness away
I can see my own screams
and monsters
I can see you leaving me

    lie down
    go back to sleep
    it's really time for me to leave

breakingout

evolving
like a virus

changing
it gets better and worse
in one breath

how do i control
myself
how do i control
this disease

don't think
just breathe
don't breathe
just bleed

don't want
just need

an average day
takes a wild turn
an average day
set off into the sky

out of the atmosphere
and into space
can't replace

another misdemeanor comes
trade me places
can't erase

wearing a mask
that says stay back

naked without
my face

cheekbones gnawed on
every day
i'm losing the ability
to see

the difference between...
////youmememeyou\\\\
RORRIM/MIRROR

where am i
who am i
delusions
delusions

she can't tell
i can't tell
where the hell
catch-22
fall-37
fly
a virus in the sky
inmyb
r
a
in
sanity
it's p
l
a
y

in
sanity

frustrated
bloodshot
oohshit
falling through
walking through walls
stalling
keep me moving

sticks and stones
words will never hurt
words will always hurt me
the words swimming around
my brain is swelling to sizes
unimaginable
EXPLODEIMPLODE
neverhowitshouldbe
thewholeworldiswatchingme

safety is lonely//safety is in numbers
safe never safe
from me

unDead last

dreaming in public
the empty inside calls to me

always in last place
it's time to entertain our guests
depression and hello-to goodbye
i always knew you were just a lie

living for the end
my cat walks away since
i don't care enough to love her
oh if only i loved life like i love you

place your hand over my heart
see, that it's not beating?
i am the worst kind of undead
i don't suck your blood
i don't suck the blood of animals
i suck the happiness out of you
you better leave before it all goes away
come back and see me when i'm breathing again

the cat comes back
i act confused
and reach out to pet her

winged undertakers

even black crows deserve not to feel so lonely
watching us, with those beady eyes

waiting for us to croak, so they can fly on by
to graveyards full of broken hearts
and lonely strangers;

we're all strangers to ourselves

even after that last breath of air
gravestones left, as we become part of the earth;
we sit, wanting only to not be forgotten

on wrought iron gates the black crows oversee
bodies finally warm with the soils
of our own trappings

they are quite comfortable with reminding the living
that breathing is only a temporary existence

but loneliness can last forever

head against the wall

words are lost
sadness takes over

i forgot what it feels like
a blade against the skin

how ridiculous
but i think it through
and let it go
i think it through
it's nothing new

Blue October soothes the soul
though the chaos still continues
but only in colours violet and grey
the angered reds are held at bay

tomorrow
i look around for something special
and leave without a sound
i'm just picturing myself as you
but maybe you already knew

standing
facing a plan
making mistakes
it's so hard to take
just let the pills take hold
and all that's left
are the lies i told

smiling, i'll let go

make it so

without a breath to take
i listen to the dull static of the seagulls on the beach
the moon dies out but the sun no longer brightens my day
my only company is a twig that ebbs and flows
in the irreclaimable time
so i walk

as i walk the wind blows
it sings a song only little creatures can understand
i wish i could understand it too
have a pleasant conversation with someone
not myself but someone else
so i think

as i think it gets colder
i zip up my jacket to block the Frost
earth's change is the only thing that matters
these human dramas mean nothing
i wish they could take a break
breathe and see
what monsters we've become
who we could be
something pretty
so i frown

as i frown
it comes to me as a dream
to make it all go away
is it the right choice to make?
do i have any pros do I have any cons?
so i smile

as i smile working

with my delusions conflicts of the mind
what i think
that someone shadows my every step
maybe paranoia will come in handy since
i may believe
i do believe
the iron fist of death dances off the reel
so i wait

as i wait
i remember how i use to wait for you
but now
now i wait for
his scythe to calm the waves

speakers and scotch tape

taping up advertisements of Rusted dreams
sometimes all one needs
is a true dose of heartache Fashion Show
it has designs suitable for season upon season
love hate disaster and fate
maybe I said this a little too late
but it's an exemption of words Without Company

ripping apart shirts like spirits
all i hear i fear and i wish
invisibles, my darlings, to take a sip
lemonade laced with medication and exploitation
it's time Things Change
it's time you leave

disbanding myself from reality
my tears an exhibit for
the destined to be blind
and for the random passersby's
looking through their dirty Glass windows

asking the Ouija board
why Liar is only me
but all i say Is Gone
memories come rushing back
and in my head there are
236 rooms to decorate
and 159 doors to nowhere
so deliberately i take the fire escape
and i Jump to check if there's any place to go
any direction to help me find my home

manic-depression

start over,
talons squeezing
making up minds

reliving lives
the smiles i remember to hide
the tears that i can't seem to fight
open up, breathing in your smell

talking back,
welcomed back into hell
convoluted,
she always said
but i always disagreed
it's just easier for me

the goblin king holding all my dreams
i just have to give up everything

what's left of me
after...
what's the best thing to say
when you ask me to stay

i won't say yes
but i can't say no
i just want you to go

you hold me captive
and i'm so tired
but i'm nothing without you

panicking, judging the highs

and judging the lows
nothing is more simple
than when i'm without you

apathetic, but i'm still breathing
candid, but i'm always lying

i'm all over the place
and it's all because of you
it's all because of

a sitcom called CRASHE

reshape me
my sight is getting hazy
these aren't hallucinations
i just have the power to see
demons and forces
that claim us that fake us
/that end us

it's a sitcom:
"help!
it's dark
and i can hear laughing"
really?
must you mock me?

it's the same

another bond
so far away
what's between
you and me?
a million miles//
a couple steps?
this is just empty...

it's the same
but it's always changing

i'm thrifty when it comes to my sanity
i think that's why i kept you around/
you were so poor, a couple dimes in my head
was like a whole piggy bank of mental health
in your eyes

madness always seemed balanced
in your eyes
i could never go wrong

so how the hell did i get here?

it's like you never
touched my skin
but there's still a scar/
a burn that will never heal

and now i can't feel the wind on my skin
without wanting to scream
my insides are squirming
i'm looking at the world
in the eyes of the cockiest worm
i have ever known

pretty bird// chirping bird,
give me purpose again...
swallow me whole
just devour me

i'm tired of dreaming

so slap me across the face
shake me like i'm crazy
just please
WAKE ME UP
reshape me
my sight is getting hazy
these aren't hallucinations...

complications

caught in the breakdown
hung up the phone
the situation heightened by
anonymous conversation
shouldn't ever be left alone

alone to think.
thinking as the ghost plays on
Gerard sings away
but though i beg
my mouth is clamped shut
too afraid to open
too afraid to scream

will it be heard
doors shut, lights are turned off
an abyss appears at the bottom
of the stairs
and the falling down...
i can see the future dimming

letting out the blood
the knives that stab me as i breathe
home is a figure of speech
that i cannot ever reach

i feel caught in the winds
grasping for tree branches
keep me stable, immobile

but mobility means no more
waiting for him, for Grim, to find me catch me
i am not wearing an invisibility cloak

but it sure as hell feels like it

it's back to chocolate milk and medication
just like before
soon, i'll add drink upon drink upon drunk stupors
but i am coping, hoping
stumbling down the road
begging for the courage
to live

begging for the courage
to die

electrolytes feed me,
electroshock needs me
self-satisfied, forget forget forget
can't remember,
how it feels, ask me the questions,
the U, S, and A
but it doesn't matter the answers
it never happened anyways

all a dream a dream
in my drink upon drink upon drunk stupors
how super

cracked.

i don't have any goals
except to leave

so i'll find myself another dead person
i'll find myself at the wake
and kneel at their coffin
whispering all my dirty secrets,
crying

for their sake
for mine
for

complications

likely a little looming leverage

like the rain
i pour my heart out
tearing up my mind
shredding up the belief
that i can get better
like the night sky
my soul is black
except for those shining smiles
that i let out once in a while
like my iPod
i play songs in my head
that only i have heard
but like a little bird
i start singing

DVD
deadly visions desired
OM[M[G
on my mother's grave
i'll tell you two little things
suicide is the only smile
the only tear
the only true feeling i get anymore

and deadly dreaming, desiring demons
visions of violent vehement vile veins
run through me
red on pale cream
dripping dripping
until

like the sun
i go down

breaking the pattern

following your footsteps
taking every wrong turn
taking every escape-from-reality detour
wonderland's worst ways
fairy tale island gone bad

misery misses me i hear
lucky for her i'm visiting again soon
to follow in your footsteps

following your footsteps
better better horrible lies they're horrible lies
i'm fine i'm fine i am lying for the best
less than normal more i'm hurting i'm hurting

mystery it's a mystery
i'm still here she says
i'm just following your footsteps a little longer
waiting for the best you say comes next
more lies more lies
i try i try i want to fly away
but i must wait just a bit longer

i am following your footsteps all the way
back to wonderland weekends
motel monsters mend my missing parts
my broken heart
turn away turn away before it's too late

i remember this day from a dream i once had
turn away turn away before it's too late
this day doesn't end well for…

someone once told me that it's too late
someone once told me i was worse than you
that i'm worse than i see myself
i don't see me ;;
i see a shadow of what i want to be
darker darker ;; ugh it's disgusting
but it's okay… i'm okay [i swear i'm not lying]
it's all alright because
today's the day i turn away

last stake

star on one side skull on the other
sitting on the floor with the laptop warming me
shut the door and close my heart up
i don't want you here today
just let me break away
i want to hear you laugh at me

whichever way not to go
i always seem to follow
my heart heavy with nails
scratch the blackboard with broken beer bottles
let my ears start ringing
thinking i'm thinking too much
whatever did i do to let you fall
i miss life un-confusing

and i let it get out of hand
but i hear you might have too
whatever happened to me and you
you think you love me
you think you care
you think you know me
you think you're there
but tell me one thing
however did you become so invisible
invisible in front of me

wishes wear me out and then
i hide under the covers
crying without you to see
you think you're so intuitive still
going over the hill
your insane past is my future it seems

and i get chills

what happens when
in the end the only friend i have hates me
and follows me around just to let me know
i'm broken i'm lost i'm everything you're not
i'm everything you are
i'm just a figment of your imagination
driven by a force unforgiving

fetal position
tears blood and poison
but you know i'm used to it
only one place left for me
just don't send me
don't let me
don't let me see
don't
think dream believe
i'll ever be any more than not okay

over and over i don't want to say
please stay help me please hate me please go away
make up my mind for me make up my mind for you
i know not to confide in you
just a twig to break in two
all right i'm alright
never forever and again
let the end be my forever friend

you and me living fancy free
don't you hear me
when i call for safety
i know you'll leave me
when all i need
is

speaking to nature

one day
talking to the cosmos

"i had no idea
that the gun was loaded"
i explain,

"i couldn't have been sure
but it seemed such a nice day
to start relaxation"

the cosmos replies,
"daughter
how do you find
a weeping willow in an apple tree?"

my answer was nothing
curiosity and confusion
- a look that said
your wisdom is aplenty,
and mine is dwindling

"by noticing the lines of stress
and the tears opening into it's heart"

i ask,
"but why does that matter?
that has nothing to do with
why i am here"

the cosmos says,
"i disagree;
no matter how much the apple tree tries

to stay making sweet apples
if any one person stops to truly taste
he will taste just a tad bit of sour
because the tree itself
feels sour and sad"

"okay..."

"you see,
i have been watching you
and you cannot trick me
like the weeping willow hiding in an apple tree
you are hiding and you are sad;
of course you knew the gun was loaded
just like you knew
what the consequence would be
when it went off"

"an end to all of the pain", i reply

"but now that you are here
what do you expect?
here there is only me and you
i can only give you so much
before the satisfaction of death
becomes a deeper longing of life;
it will get lonely"

the cosmos opens my body up
and shows me my grief
and gives me the relaxation i was searching for
but then
gives me a taste of the pain to come
i fall to my knees asking,
"should i return to my other life?"

"you must make that decision
on your own
but be weary;
if you wait too long to decide
there is a chance you may not reenter"

"if i choose to,
how do i get back?"i wonder

"by opening your eyes"
the cosmos whispers

switch course

i search the closet
and find exactly what i've been looking for
i take my German army jacket
get my bag of clothes
grab my keys off of the counter
and head out the door

twelve in the morning
no cars pass mine
i take a left on 131st so it seems like i know
which course to take-
but i don't even know where i'm driving to
-having direction is not the point of this journey
let the road guide me to where i need to go

the snow glides gracefully down from the sky
i'm surprised the ozone layer hasn't opened up enough that
God falls into earth's atmosphere
making him burn and boil from his own stupid mistake
of giving people free will

i laugh-
there is no fucking God
oh, if my former friend was here now
I'd get just another lecture
just another hateful look
she was, is, and will always be
a Jesus lover with absolutely no religious humor
-especially from an atheist like me

my stomach craves coffee
so i turn into Starbucks parking lot-
the place looks closed

and i check a little closer just to make sure::
the door says it closes at eleven
-dammit

i go back to my car and
turn on the radio
i find nothing of interest
switch it to the cd player
listen to the emo etiquette
of how to:: slit the wrists
and Kill Hannah
i crank it up
the red mini lighter is out again
dancing with my last cigarette
playing hard to get
all it matters is if i get my freedom::
four minutes of half bliss
and half nicotine nightmares
the knots in my back untie
and i smile

i pull over for gasoline
more cigarettes
and a shitty cup of coffee
-caffeine shots
how i miss what used to be
-i wish i knew where i'm going

i lowered my self-esteem again
began to cut deeper and deeper into my skin
-my soul
every fucking day
i'm not eating anymore
just withering away
drinking vodka straight

every day after work
pot and crank rule my life
half of my fucking income
goes to my addictions
i fucking hate it

it still isn't the same
i told you from now on
I'll never need you
i told you from now on
I'll always be okay
i'm surprised you didn't catch me in the lie
you used to do so well
but i wonder, is it that you're getting worse at finding the lies
or is it that i'm better at making them?

i look like shit today
withdraw
my fucking dealer died
got shot by some asshole
not wanting to pay
fuck
where the hell am i supposed to get
my neutral noose?

i take a left onto a gravel road
alone, a worn house rests fitfully
with graves and broken windows
i stop the car, keep it running,
and walk behind the empty house
to see what i can find
-a cliff
splashing water
rocks
damage
erosion

my journey is over
i close my eyes
and-

from the other side

*"Dear Loving Nightmare,
don't forget me
when I leave
don't worry
it only seems
like eternity"*

go away little girl
I won't break down
not today, not here
facsimile: not tomorrow, not there
it's only eternity

out of control, a grin so wide
it's time to make those
who hurt me cry
and everyone knows it's great to be
swallowed up in jealousy

taking a walk
letting the dust settle
old photographs
letters and memories
left behind in plastic boxes
I'm not going to check
if they still have a hold on me
instead, just ignite

new life
striving to be better than
anything she could be
telling everyone her ugly idiosyncrasies
exploitative? no, it's only

being competitive

"Dear Hated Dream,
I didn't forget you when you left
I remember you, leaving me with nothing
only the knowledge that somewhere out there
you thought there was something better than me
you were wrong; and now you're alone
but don't worry,
it only seems like eternity"

hopeless

one little break
that's all I need
take a trip to anywhere
as long as I'm not here

I can't stay locked up,
scared of living day to day
I'm breathing dirty air
I can't pretend I'm doing well
every minute of every goddamned day
I just want to walk away

feel the anguish breach
the skin has opened and there's no blood
no lesion of any kind
you can't see,
I can barely see
but I can feel it
digging into me

just let me go
take a drive
and come back in a couple days' time
it's not like
I'm making headway here,
I'll be back by next week,
maybe next month
surely before next year
I just have to rid myself of fear

one present

one phrase
beaten and bruised
fell
"i love you" went to Hell
hate resides in my manic phase
make sure you stay away

one day
cried and confused
perusing the pages of my diary
what did you expect to find-
the time and place
or the tune and the race?
i think you got lost

one breath contaminated and claustrophobic
heart beat beat beat
faster faster
blue and green walls
with a zebra jacket
curtains ripped apart on the floor
here there are no doors
stuck

one little present
one open window
one way free
one jump away
and one last scream

under upheaval/ black morning risen

sipping on traveling thoughts
time extraterrestrial
i almost feel regret, for you,
but then i remember
and it slips away

another long ago actor
that is overlooked,
a slight smell left over
like cigarettes and stupidity--
you are washed away

the winds have spoken:
they no longer hear your sad melody
as days go on, a
broken back as the only evidence
a life ever existed
before alone

but was always lonely
"connect to me
my soul is searching
i am true, and we are one"
finding forever in
the eyes of liars

corny, lined with coke
always/never the last words spoke
missing syllables, things i wish i could let go
i heave and gag, with only
cloaked disorder left to choke

joy, given up

jokes, given away
the TV show is dim,
black and white now turns grey
as your famous lead
drifts into yesterday

empyrean demons

who am i going to tell?
i let everyone think
i've finally left my hell
sure; i've left my hell
but the smell...
the smell of bodies burning
just won't go away

cut off my head and watch my body
flop around like a fish out of water
i'm ripe for the pickin'
i just don't want to wait any longer
all i need is to be emotionally free

but freedom comes with a price
i think freedom sounds quite nice
but if not, death will suffice;
can't wait 'til i feel fever and not ice
so sad i'm cold; so manic i'm bold
it's all just the roll of the dice

manic depressive
i'm grounded
i'm   drowning
schizophrenic
i'm surrounded
they've bound me

...if i'm so happy
why do i feel like crying?
...if i love life
why do i feel like dying?
...if i can do this

why do i think i'm lying?

hand me a rope to hang from...
i don't want to die,
i was told it'd get me high
i don't want to be so numb
/give me a vice and i'll get by

this here's a stick up
my mind is a terrorist and a victim
either way,
it never shuts the fuck up

take my pills
supposedly i'll chill
but i'm down for the count
and i'm too afraid to get back up
i'm not cross, i'm just lost

come on, help me out here:
let me know that you're proud of me
even though you won't call me
i can go it alone i just need to know
that it's not my fault
that your love comes only
in a past participle

i'm strong enough to get through
but i'm not strong enough to keep you
i'm brave enough to stay
but i'm not brave enough to walk away

what do i need
to love this breath
whom must i call
to save me from this fall

tonight i'm strong enough
tonight i'm brave enough
to stand up tall

it doesn't matter my height
i'll be strong tonight
can't keep me from
reiterating "Open to Life"
life/death : death/life
here we go again tonight..

liars

a naked secret
a young ghost

the voice is liquid
concrete; ferocious
I listen; I lie

morning lingers
yesterday is poison
the universe remembers
fire and porcelain sky

harbored harmony

sitting in the ymca wearing a cheerless face
longing for an end to this disheveled beginning
Blue October's words comfort me in my time of need
i'm always in need

this product is licensed to a heart full of broken
and i laugh for nothing goes as it should
are my thoughts in order?
do i say the right thing?
is my disguise working?
as the snow starts pouring

just a teenage mess
look me in the eye and tell me
is "i love you" just a lie?

wearing blue jeans and a black hoodie
it doesn't matter how many layers i put on
i'm still cold

my treatment brewing
just a couple shocks
that's all i need
to make a smile
to proceed
with my perpetual disease

anticipating a grey morning suffering through a great warning
i am a stranger to your desires
i try to be friendly but boy they make me tired
i'm told it's just a game they play
maybe time will begin today

hands shaking
i hold my head in my hands and pretend
that this

this is the end

green sweatshirt walking

new barbed wire anklets
poisoned
veins carry fallacy through me
stumbling stars and drunken darlings
kiss me alive
rip me medical
shred me emotional
disabled
leave me empty
amble to ancient abilities
anxiously aware
you hold my heart dyed
tip me over
tea pot that will scream
dazzled dreams down (drown)
new barbed wire bracelets
skin sleazy and opened
cellar doors sing
hallucinations wring my blood dry
on cue
cursive letters let you free
last journal entry
new barbed wire necklaces
nooses for the nobody in me
an anti-hero for my own tilted novel
my own story
drunken stars and stumbling darlings
darkened corners
kiss me dead
it's over and under
me

this feels like a suicide mission

on the edge
eyes closed
breeze scarcely there
whispering

don't want to know
all this, it just
feels like falling
all this, it's just
me stalling

fighting

consequences
here taking over
there giving up
looking around
no direction
is
simple

borderline star

-a collaboration

Ashtrays overfill with addiction's last breath and
Glass on the floor lives to hurt another innocent victim

Here we are, drowning to float and falling to fly
Living (dying) for all the sins we cling to
It's like ivy strangling the beauty that was hidden inside
Covered so no one will ever see what it could have been

We make misery look like a dream
coughing up common sense like blood
Throwing it away like yesterday's paper
And it could have been so stunning

Low self-esteem assured, it's another shattered mirror inside
Just another mess to bleed over again
Remake the lie- add in pop-tarts, lemonade and razorblades
Circle of secrets. Let's all share. One too many for me
Veiled as a statue, look and see innocence is empty
No life visible - dead eyes stare back at me

Photographs write a story I wish I remembered
Brings back pain that I know I should forget
Don't I wish that tomorrow was more than a threat

Dark expectations sometimes better than reality
A dance with fangs and acid,
another manic episode and we're passed it
A curse and a smile come on and we'll stay awhile,
in the night
And here it comes,
Climax with sunshine

Here we go again
Cosmo in the room and cobra starship on the mind
Bipolar midnight with just one match
Blow it out and watch it burn
Confusion without concern
I wish it were true
Another cigarette and the ashtray falls
Shut down
And the glass cracks

number three

sleeping through the summer's winter
waiting for my veins to *POP*
for the world's tossing and turning to just *STOP*
haven't you heard the lies
they always meant for it to be okay
never did they realize something for tomorrow
may be better for today

documented emotion that stays in the corner collecting dust
i don't remember why i started but by now
it's just randomized demise routinely goodbyes
continuations of something writ yesterday's ago
i coulda swore i used this line before
a quilt of theories made different by the same ideologies
logically improbable idealistically possible
something has to go right when everything else's going left

what's the purpose what's the cause
of another humiliating endeavor of better
than ever but worse than before
nothing i say-write-believe- makes sense
but i do anyway because it gives a certain sense of security
i shouldn't trust it though it'll just end up killing me

this is number three in everything
sometimes number four
but never number two
i wonder why i wonder
why is it always nevers and forevers
confused and used
changed and always the same
always always always
not today ;; not today

this time i swear i mean it
this time i swear i believe it
this time i swear i won't change my mind
i'll prove it to you with the slices in my skin
hell it's always been that way
makes it true at least for another day

quicker than before but worse than ever
i rant and rant onto forever but never make any
argument worth ranting
never say a cross-eyed version of creative prospect
how pathetic useless
a penny to a rich man
a checkbook to a poor man
a girl to a conceited man
a chicken to a thrill-seeking girl
a nervous breakdown to me

[xxxx] as different to each other as ipods are to swastikas
not even in the same idea can't compare
apples to oranges they said
but i do
apples are sweet and oranges sour

nothing makes sense except me beside you

No Title Necessary, But It's Still a Good Accessory

I'm like an attic
with cobwebs everywhere
always cold and cluttered
and shadows that will scare

I'm like an attic
a place where unwanted memories are stored
when you aren't willing to throw them away
but don't need them anymore

I'm like an attic
the part of the house no one goes into
unless already angry or blue
sometimes they go to hide from the pain
and sometimes they go to worsen the shame

I'm like an attic/always on top
but at least I'm not like a basement

stages of sight

closed eyes trying to breathe
so ready to leave
followed by i-know-what
secrets and a side of low self esteem
i'm so glad i didn't say a thing
that the knife was so near the salivating socket
that i'm so ready to pull the plug
how the insanity does grow
it's a weed
the last fatal disease
opened eyes failing to need
blood smeared love note
decorate me in diamond spears
i don't wish to have
anything but
the story-book ending

bachelors bewitched

royal realities reason with
exemplary explosions
while bipolar breathes in the incense
in sense i don't have
give me a cent every time you say
goodbye

the Simpsons watch sincerely
as Martha Stewart bitches out everybody
and my best friend thinks she's horrible
i try to set her straight
it's turning out to be a great night without life
and without you
i'm streaming happy tears
and lies at goodnight

dead by the tree
it's another of my philosophies
turn meat to maggots
sun of the universe [son of the universe]
such a kleptomaniac taking mirrors from the store
throwing them to the floor
maniacal laughter recapture
emotional hosts

take a bite of my heart again
throw it in the trash bin
i'm dead by morning
and no one's in mourning
bruises all over
cures for cancer in a can
conversations with another man
fainting philosophical

painting personality
dire dreams and tired fiends

what's your hurry?
gin rum vodka and whisky
dive down your insides
feel so warm yes your eyes do smile
come stay awhile and break me some more
all it takes is one more break
and i'll spill over spine scorched in vein [vain] vacations
dripping blood all over the sticky floor
it's amazing to an open door
walking all over my bones
it's time to wake up and die

gypsy

cold nights
starving for a break
hands searching for rewards
never coming

it's a hopeful day
crashing below the waves
on the shore, i see
the movement backwards
is sometimes the movement forwards

sincerely trapped
but the door is open
secreting the ideal that everything is fine
i take a blade to my wrist

can't resist
revealing hide-outs
to make you miss me
more than ever
we are together
beyond the sunrise

without the gage of time
i remit the weakness
and overcome
in seconds, days
years
i become

bound up in
freedom

so funny, closed but no closure

emotions quilted
a pattern of relief and distress
at least it's over
he's going to freak
...but at least it's over

...[so funny,
it's so funny
the door's closed
but there's no closure]...

can't take it
leaving in a body bag
i'm leaving in a body bag
closed my eyes
erased, i erased/
traced veins
closing the openings
comingbackfromthedead

sitting down
watching my life continue
speeding away
all that i control
crumbles
...the castle crumbles

movement
taking all
changed
changing
change

i swallowed my heart
when it came back up,
i swallowed whiskey
when i felt empty,
i swallowed TNT
when i couldn't take another drink
i swallowed my breath
when

i thought i knew, but mood rings never lie

contortioned cries like lullabies
rest upon deaf ears
sealing destinies
with nowhere to go

cherishing the moments
forgotten dreams awaiting /awakening
i still think /i still hear salvation calling
but no one answers

when

i ask for stability
a mind that will not break
i cover myself with
dirt, and no one can see

frightening the urge...
fragments of objects sharper than words
sink into skin
scarlet pain drips and remembers

loveless

a sadness starts
reaching towards
an end that won't forget
that even after /that evening after
long forgotten

this chapter lies open
going nowhere

life surrounds me lying still
the rain no longer falls;
without creaking boards and footsteps in the halls,
my ghosts don't ever wake;
my heart no longer beats;
and the bed sheets never warm
my body through the thunderstorms

reoccurring...

it's all just
a disaster waiting to unfold...
secrets still creeping up, left untold
but watchful

leaving

when the monsters tenderly stroke your hands, hair and back
to welcome you back to...
this is the ode to
unknowingly /so very knowingly

nonexistent

covered

the rain falls sideways as
my unlucky red lighter
jumpstarts my heart
like a car with too much wear

everything outside is grey except
a red balloon floating away
i decide to clean my room of everything
with meaning -without-
but i still feel dirty

red foil-wrapped kisses
hate me for unwrapping them
and throwing them away
i'm tired of poisonous chocolate lies

woodchips from my desk
stick to my pants
afraid to let go and fall-
they remind me of
everyone i've ever known

a red Coke can
sits, open and empty
unwanted- for it's been violated
having its value
sipped away

the rocking chair in the corner
stays immobile but warm-
a throw cover blankets its
loneliness like
my smile does to my fear

the room feels ugly
with marks scattered across the walls-
pale cream with its purpose
still unseen ;; it's being
taken advantage of
like so many who's walked its hall

the internet connection is weak
as red tears spill out from my pen
my lighter fails to start my heart
as i look out the window again
the red balloon is nowhere to be seen
and everything is still so grey

view 6

lay down the law
Lucifer gave me this gun
told me to go ahead and have some fun
maybe i'll go on the killing spree that i've been talking about
wipe out the human race except for a couple girls
and i'll shoot the sperm
and fetuses will go to hell right along with me
maybe i'll just shoot you
save you from my love
live and you just might see
the invisible pretty inside of me
maybe i'll just make pretend
hide the gun until the twenty-second
march march march
April, wake up honey it's time you feel
the schizophrenic side of me
everyone wants to see
what she told them i have
everyone wants to leave
because of what she told them
let's just pretend this gun is filled with water
let's just pretend i'd never do it again
let's just pretend
maybe i'll let it go
maybe i'll forgive the psycho
hey it's cocked and ready
didn't you hear the sound
you told me i'd start the chain
honey you don't know
i'm too far gone to care
guilt trip to keep me alive
thanks guys
maybe i'll just wipe you out

maybe i'll just

i'll just kill **M**ary **E**mbers
and she'd be so happy
to breathe again
to sigh
to take the gun to her head
baby it's just ME
baby it's just a Movie Ending

this is an outstanding POS

this is life
standing between humility and humiliation
it's plain to me
that I stand for everything
nothing
I am not real
whatever I feel I never felt before
none of this is real

standing between fuck you and please save me
falling down but afraid to get picked back up
take away all the sin in the world
and what's left?
jealous of the empty girls
who walk around with hollow laughs
who am I to say that everything will turn out okay?

standing between stranger and danger
don't know which way to turn
the world flies by so fast
have you ever wondered about the masks?
no one's safe from the pain
shove it in my face and tell me I've never felt before
that I don't know what it is to cry
baby, you know that's a fucking lie
I live and die because of feeling
but trust me, I'm dealing
while invisible razors split my skin
I can feel the blood pouring
didn't you see me
I don't think the disease is real
I just think I was a mistake
I can't take me back

but you can push until I crack
when I have no one to turn to
and everything is out of whack
I promise I won't fight back

if you're meant to die
you're going to die
that's the final destination
but go ahead
write your hate, your pain, your fucking shame all over me
with knives dull but sharp enough to open me
let me be the one you come to when you're done
let me be the one to care when no one else is there
let me be the one who'll fix you and your broken dreams
who'll make you think of all those things unseen
let me be the one to break

standing not even five feet tall
on a bridge ready to fall
I won't be there if you call
don't ask me why
cuz I'm not sure I know
but I'm just afraid if I stay
I won't ever know how and where to go
can you take it all away?
I won't ask you that today
out loud, anyway
I don't think you realize
but this may be my hearts demise

this is life
I'm breaking up
I'm falling down
but this time you won't be around
I just wished you would be the one
to let me drown

sea legs on a plane

a star on the bottom of a translucent cup-

a plane without the peanuts-

another place where i miss the old days.
fasten your seat belts please,
we're ready for take-off.

broken-hearted chucks
walk across multicoloured carpet,
hesitate on aisle seven, seats F E and D
sit down with an exasperated sigh.

fasten your seatbelts please,
we're ready for take-off.

take off your mask please,
anonymity does not work here.
hide away from the world under black bangs.
look out the window but don't look down,
don't look down.

fasten your seatbelts please,
we're ready for take-off.

don't puke please,
from thoughts of glorious plane destruction
and only one mortal wound ;;
from shivers from shakes ;;
from too much to drink ;;
from derelict dreams ;;
from another dismal day ;;

fasten your seatbelts please,
we're ready for take-off.

off the plane already,
two hours of writing and
music blaring salvation into my ears.
walk through the airport with a
sense that something has gone wrong.
[something always goes wrong.]

fasten your seatbelts please,
we're ready for take-off.

follow the leader please.
get picked up by a familiar stranger,
pretend life is going well,
going in the right direction
"are we driving in the right direction?"
"home is only miles away."
and i mutter in response
"home is not that way."

fasten your seatbelts please,
we're ready to crash.

Prozac attack

oval answers and anesthesia working wonders
keeping everything in
break the cycle
let them have a shoot up
at gunpoint all you care about
is the thought :: shoot me shoot me
let me free from this physical tragedy
blood seeps through
bleed blue
no one will remember you
triangles
thoughts behaviors emotions
you fought the saviors
echolocation
the bat's Prozac
the wrong time for
normal
formal ballroom dancing
romance suffocating
stabbed in the back
blood seeps through
no one will remember you
squares
you swear on
morphine and good mornings
shaky stars chocolate bars and heroin scars
hide away the needle tray
don't you want to hide away?
lose the blood
heavy heavy heavy
breathe heave puke need
to relocate veins
heroin addiction

stuck it in wrong
needle is too strong
blood seeps through
no one will remember you
circles
just circles
of remade mistakes
get your mind in shape
it seems you're obsessed with these
so break free
break free pull the reins
stop before you go insane
slit the wrists as a last resort
you should know i'll have to retort
you'll have a long stay in hell
ring the bell the bellman will take your bags
and throw them in the fire
you won't need material desires
razor sharp hexagons
it seems you didn't learn a thing
you ended your life and now
blood seeps through
but i will remember you

awake and sleeping

rotten tricks and killing mice
snow drops in globs down the chimney
the air is flat and my vault is gone
i wish i wasn't so dirty all the time
drinking everything in sight
let's go up and start a fight
scratches on my face from just another taste
left bleeding in the corner
inside bruises
give me an instructional video on how to fuck
your diary opens only to me
i hide in your cartoon thoughts
it's just broken plates
pirated
naked
dead penguins grin
where is what yesterday is
walk on by with your beautiful lies
walk on by with your pretty eyes
squeaky clean let me lie
i'm so clean now don't you know
you don't know a thing
intervention it's too late
go masturbate
yeah you know i hate
i can't love
i can't make it
sewing my heart back together
chocolate breakfast
taste it down and it comes right back up
inflate balloons it's too soon
salt shaker it burns my burns
my cuts

just another false line
eat the words you never said
you never said truthfully
bend your knees
kneel to me
bastards don't deserve a thing
i don't deserve a thing
pop the balloons
born broken
too heavy
i fall
trust is fucking gone
i'm
dead

dirty pop and TNT [time<u>BOMB</u>]

see through
through walls of trust that never were
see redemption
you'll never get
much more than hazy
it's all but broken
my wrist is dressed in red today
i stare in admiration
beauty dressed in blood
i walked around in nothing but lies
sat down
green couch swallowing me to watch the other
aol.video another voice cries
just again
a static surprise
there's nothing left to hear
screaming through the night
the dark consumes
and my hallucinations dance around and play
though i fear
i fear so much
but i don't fear
i don't fear you
i don't fear dying
smiling
"little sister calling"-
the lost boys soundtrack loving
time changes
the day always stays the same
the night never passes through
i see through you
barely anything but broken
heart hazy through contacts

cons attack
you were
always will be
conned conning
honed straight on me
but leaving
mind contorting
saved but dead
nothing compares to you
wrist dressed in red again
stomach dressed in white white white red blue white
pants of pills
chills
then thrills
end it all on a good day
alive but barely
i missed you
alive but dead
i still miss you
i'm still

dear Lightning

your veins shedding,
tearing through the patchy fabrics of sky:
clouds pondering the existence of why
while their tears always falling with realistic wry

a limitless light, purple or white
your beauty just mesmerizes
but your brother still analyzes
believing noise is a determined voice

but blood pours from the ears
as creaky stairs remember
past lovers
and past lovers remember
staying warm through thunderstorms

he boasts about being the host:
having a storm named after him
but secretly, you know his strength is slim
as he is just a warning for
you in mourning

and i watch you
how you go across the sky
magistrate hello-goodbye
nothing before you, or after

could have done this to me
only you had the power;
i am on my knees begging

tame the storm incarnate
all of your family

flowing as my bloodstream
it is no longer necessary
for the thunder in me to scream

i want to be so silent,
a quiet simple form
of the beauty of the storm

i want to be you
no longer me, i want your destiny
seconds lasting
that's all i'm asking
i just want to survive time
a never-forgotten nursery rhyme

i just want to survive.

without

and a new old begins
recognizing forgotten glances
the smells and tastes of
what yesterday was,
and could have been:

i wake to phone calls
falling back asleep to
autumn's whisper

conscious of the terror,
the trembling in my body
i can't help but think
all the meanings of "without"

but i attempt...
contemplating contentment
as words of another bring
me closer and closer
to the grave

the hole is ready
already holding many
precious memories,
and old loves

though they may have forgotten me,
or walked another path, freely
i do not forget them,
always keeping a place
at the table, a place in my heart
for if ever they decide to return

i sit in time,
watching ghosts pass
weakened by the things unsaid

and here, in every moment that i let pass
another beat of my heart
brings me to a colder home

a place in the cemetery
where my name already lies;
where many already decompose

just like me, they were terrified
to live their lives to the fullest
and now they pay their debts
for eternity

but what i would do
for that one perfect day
that one perfect moment
that could make me realize

i don't have to be afraid
because this moment
loved me

and that's all i've ever asked for

sunken treasure

fixating on the hole residing in my soul-
is it possible to fix life when every decision
you make feels like the wrong one?

winning a losing battle
sacrificial stories about
counterfeit love and self-belittlement
if i give up anything good that could come
will you let me fall into a real-life dream?

my words mean nothing
as the owl in the woods
keeps asking who who who
who do i believe
mean everything to me
and why i just continue to let them leave

stomach bleeding from the inside out
while suffering from diseases that
don't really exist
and an insatiable desire
to retire into oblivion
and never wake again

damaged goods
swinging back and forth
trying to reach the sky
and find a reason
to believe in the existence
of good conquering evil

what is evil?
just a misconceived ideal

that went astray
a love presented in a forgiven forgotten
last meal, that can't reveal
hidden dreams
confusion no less than
dementia in a soup of
ugly hallucinations

this couldn't have been
less cliché,
a wedding with a dead bouquet
this couldn't have been
a better day
ending it with the thunderstorm
the clouds and the lightning
my fear heightening
but it's just another secret
just another lie
i will keep tonight

i want to be hidden in the stars

i want to feel beautiful again
with the blade against my skin
pressing, pressing in
bleeding the emptiness,
bleeding the sin
i want to feel beautiful again

i want to be someone
someone known by the world
gossiped about in all the hotels
suppressing all my addictions
managing all my suppressions
all in one, two, three, ten
fucking pills baby,
it's not self-medication
if your doctor says it's okay

i want to be the whore
the whole world would want to stroke
with every hit of any-everything, with every snort of coke
i'll be that confident whore
the whole world would want to stroke
but no one would love
no one would love

i want to be something other than crazy
something better,
some creative form of acid-induced, ADD imagery
it's okay to be manic-depressive
as long as
as long as
it's worth it to feel
this fucking unreal

is it worth it to feel?

i want to be hidden in the stars
so someone would always call me pretty
looking up at the heavens
asking why i'd never believe they're more than
a fake history, made to create chaos and love
all in one fantastic, all in one fantastic dream
it's all a dream
all a dream
to make death seem just a bit more pretty
just like the stars, the stars i see
every time i look into your eyes i see
i see the heavens

i want to be more than a hallucination
you fell in love with once,
and minutes later found someone real
existing in your nation of naked nuisances
to be close enough to feel the fire burning in your eyes
become dismantled and fall
straight into your final goodbye
you said hello, and i smiled
it was your final lie

i want to be alright
when the world ends and all that's left
is me and the society i created in my head,
hoping one of them would realize
that i am good enough
i wish i was good enough
to open up, to be me
so everyone would know
everyone would know
bliss is dismissed and inside me the demon hides-
there are so many secrets

that i've never ever said

i want to be beautiful again
i want to be someone
i want to be the whore
i want to be something other than crazy
i want to be hidden in the stars
i want to be more than a hallucination
i want to be alright
i want to be
i want to stop dreaming
i want to start believing
i want to start living
it doesn't matter, so instead

i want to be dead.

racing

slumber in silence
snort sacrilegious
short fuse ceremonious
an almost end
backwards friend

tear the wall paper
spray paint the lies
a neon surprise
anonymous goodbye
unintelligent

wanted
with a u and an n
a prize for my seizure
so come catch me lucky charms
all up in my head
pot of gold for fools

run away
marriage to the stowaway
invisible to
stomach cries out for help
anxiety taking all to save
empty bottles i wish were still full
no halves of pessimistic voice change
erase

burn
like the back of my hand
both forearms
emotional dead end
apathetic warns

shards and splinters trapped
caught police and doughnuts

every other choice
record record recorded
one call retorted
bunnies and zombies suffocate
illusions delusions
show and tell

tumble down
rip apart
release me from my internal prison
first to break
that time to wake
mourning funeral for
ultimate outcomes
finality

break/through, a symphony in two parts

moments after a brilliant night
a standing ovation in my heart
my smile doesn't fade

it's after nightfall
and i'm with you.

my spirit connecting
with all whom i love
if they notice or not
these bonds are
stronger than titanium

and

these times are mine to remember
like a polaroid; a snapshot of life
clear, like an undisturbed pond
i respond to this life
with a determination i thought lost
;
creating a space
of true peace,
i am chaos balanced
with only hours before i leave this place
to hear the sound of perfection
giving me direction

Ohio here i come,
to bask somewhere new
with this fresh-cut lawn view
i think i'll fall in love,
it's true

i think i'll fall in love
with the sky
never once looking back
never once asking why
i think i'll fall in love...

the open road ahead
giving me hope.

i can achieve
if i breathe in
and out again;
if i breathe in

expecting, accepting
i am free
if only i just let myself be

time to sleep,
i just wonder if
tonight,
life will finally be better
than my dreams

there's a time and place for everything

a wave of consciousness hiding
under the world comes a blanket:
lies covering insecurities
and long sleeves concealing self-injuries

a room of mirrors
all distorted, but all showing what I really am
misconstrued with loud silences holding me true
/
but I keep my eyes closed, trying to hold in tears
breathing out and in and in and out
pretending to let go of yesterday
no longer living there;
there where you hear blinding lights
and see screaming voices

but here
here I find shadows
shadows that never lie when I see
monsters and wilted flowers
shadows that whisper to me
about the bitter end
and the sound a dying bird makes

; but
the confusion the illusion
it's too much to swallow
so let's shoot the bullet into my brain
let the words I wrote tomorrow remain
but before I say it I'll bite my tongue
and take the oxygen from my lungs

I will

cut my heart out, giftwrap it carefully
Fedex it straight to your door-
make sure the letter says
Merry Christmas this time
I hope you won't ignore-
this present was hard to find, I hid it in the floor
This once was mine but now it's yours

and here I am walking straight into my grave
before saying I love you yesterday

un-adapted

bind me until all that's free is your mind
mine is already tied
in knots and thoughts
lots of left turns and "i got lost"
i got so lost

as snakes suffocate my will to live
you made your own bed
now sleep like the dead
snakes still suffocate and surround
let the screaming resound

read my words
and decide in your head-
maybe out loud
it doesn't matter anyhow-
am i normal or little miss turmoil
is this a fantasy or the real world you didn't see
you didn't believe

mad hatter
tears and laughter
batter up
here's the pitch
leave me lifeless -soulless- in a ditch
Hell is prettier than this old witch

smile and realize
this
this is the End

a foundation for failure

it should be so easy
natural:
breathing

i can't let go
holding my breath
to feel

i'm alive, they say
i'm alive, i say
there's no other way
to hurt this much

but you know me,
i can't be easy
on myself, always demanding the best
but expecting the worst
i can never be forgiving
in this dilemma, you know me
at least that's what i used to believe

plastic faces
looking in on me
taking pictures
of insecurity

insecurity...
but still put on a pedestal
higher than the heavens/
held to the highest of standards

i held my breath
not wanting to disappoint

trying to keep my cool
really, just being a fool

stuck stuck stuck
[glued to you]
i couldn't come down,
but i had a pretty view:
i could see for miles
all the damaged pedestals
from your past

i asked why you put me up here
you told me i'd never disappoint
that i was perfect,
even with my shortcomings

do you still believe that today
or did i fall back to earth--
or even down to hell?
plummeting back to society
them looking up/
now looking down
pavement caressing a deadly head wound
i thought it was so easy
natural
to breathe, now i don't think at all

i forfeit my right
to love

mistrust, misthought

somewhere inside of me
is a land where i long to be
a place where smiles reside
and i don't feel the need to hide

but here, lost in a place i've never been
regrettably, in a place i somehow remember
the words i write sing songs in my head
sad melodies without happy endings

how do i know that everything's okay
when it's not?
how do i smile
when the tears keep falling?

above me stars are lost in someone's eyes
maybe tomorrow they will remember
where they belong
but maybe they do belong in the eyes of the pretty
but maybe the whole idea is just petty

i have no control over the stars,
and sometimes it's almost as if i have no control over me
i try my best
but somehow always lack
somehow i always fall back
into the world of
disaster

who am i
where am i
am i falling
or flying

i close my eyes
and all i find
is an irrational mind

thoughtless
i will tell you lies
just to make it all seem nice
i will tell you lies
to make me believe
that my heart isn't ice
that half a smile will suffice

i won't lie
i can't seem to say goodbye

arsenal assets

sitting duck in the big city
hoarse from hoarding too many heroes
apparently they're all zero's
so i sleep slap breathe that
poised poisoned posies
we all fall down
drowning in the crowd
i can't make a sound
clap contort to the last resort
don't forget the ECT
extra careful triggers
get a better gun and let love die
when did Dead become so happy?
sinking into fertile soil
soft like a pillow
smells like cinnamon
heard like a mockingbird
thinks like a genius
tastes like sweet honey
my destiny lies under dandelions
dragging my brains behind me
catching diseases wherever i go
terminally ill with ignorance
don't give me a bloody chance
all i'll do is stab the romance
the hills are blind
and i need comfort
metal chairs fit for a prisoner
prisoner of the mind
look over me
it's invisibility darling
bold and underlined
which word is most important here?

would it make sense to you?
sleepwalking to the streets
eyes walking through the sheets
it was only the man dancing
dancing the salsa alone in my bedroom
will i exist like my figments in the morning?
would you remember me when you wake up
and find yourself
a sitting duck in the big city?

courage in tour [escaping entourage]

last is always first
break down
tires slit the hearse is it
make it back home soon
the sun hides resides in lies
the clouds speak gloom
raining suicide notes

first is always falling
swinging make it to the sky
swing set crashes to the ground
drowning in rust
you've lost my trust
tape it with ducks quack it with bad luck
throw bread to the dead

falling is never at the end
resent memories tossed salad
lettuce let us infect salmonella
egg us on with black silk umbrellas
hold my hand and let me drop
sea is watching over me
diving into sound

end dances slowly
sequins start the love
hearts play on scream tell me what you mean
favorite colour is the queens disease
scene the last of that nasty fall
let it go to hell prey tell
feast on the beasts goodnights
moon sinks into the dream

slowly veins go insane
whats left to remain nothing left is great
change my taste
cigarettes sigh and breathe and lie
believe nothing nothing nothing
nothing ever goes right
everything is ending tonight
unfold the equation
displace the confusion
illusion illicit image invisible
contact the blurry
innocent bystander beguiled
one last empty smile

tic tac toe

cyanide sipping
dreams fill my eyes with the lies you always told

  drinking a monster
  feeling it corrode my very soul
  whatever can i do to be
  antithetic of the monster you see

i long to be something different-
the ink is gone from my pen
so i fill it with the blood from my arm
slicing and dicing until you can play tic tac toe
four times over

pills pills pills
give me one more pill
i think that one more
just one
may stop the thriving grief inside of me

i swallow the pills
take a swig of monster
and let go of all that i ever was-

Caroline Ashe is a thing of the past

the alchemist

and down it goes,
flailing my arms,
trying to grab on to anything;
something that could
create the miracle
sabotage the disaster
bubbling up inside

and the cork flies
swallowing the pain
i cannot understand
watching you behind closed 'lids
comprehending a broken soul
complimenting a liar's truth

and i shake
resisting the urge
do not make me
i cannot find the will to be
anything more than what you see
here, in the corner

talking fast, just nonsense building
holding close Albert
loved for years
but he no longer knows me as well
as the soft polar bear

tipping, iceburg dead ahead
but we cannot turn
we dread and dread
the awful wish of death
but can we turn it off?

not in this head, not in this head

soaring through
one last kiss, and i'll say ado
where do i go from here but up?
but
down

down

down

razors sharpened and fingers intact
this is my fire's love turned Ashe
goodbye my dream; this is my
final act

close to THE END

i let an ending be my beginning
the darkness swallowed me up
a black abyss that called me darling
i was home only if i was in your arms–
but i never was

i let a Christmas tree tell me which way to go
after you i had no home
Christmas presents under the tree
wrong house wrong presents wrong me
so pathetic, infinitely

my throat is scratchy from puking up
all my fairy tale ever after dreams
every memory i ever had with you
every time i told someone the words "i love you"
all my meals from just another sad day
i need a better getaway

i'm so confused
i don't know which way's up
and surely which way's down
am i cold? am i hot?
surely not?
but whatever it's just another failed attempt
at being pretty

i can't speak
i'm so weak
pale and i can't think
breaking dishes to hear the noise
tired of your voice running rampant in my mind

i can't find an exit
all i need is a fire escape
and i'm gone
no need to see me anymore
i'm wasted, tired; just a liar
i need the end without the gore
i can't stand this anymore

www.ingramcontent.com/pod-product-compliance
Lightning Source LLC
Chambersburg PA
CBHW022305060426
42446CB00007BA/594